CHUCK WAGON COOKBOOK

CHUCK WAGON

COOKBOOK

by Beth McElfresh

With an Introduction by Joseph C. O'Mahoney
Former United States Senator from Wyoming

SAGE BOOKS
Swallow Press / Ohio University Press
Athens

© Copyright 1960 by Beth McElfresh

Library of Congress Cataloging-in-Publication Data
McElfresh, Beth.
Chuck wagon cookbook/by Beth McElfresh : with an introduction by
Joseph C. O'Mahoney.
p.   cm.
Originally published 1960.
ISBN 0-8040-0042-5
1. Cookery, American—Western style.   2. Outdoor cookery.
I. Title.
TX715.2.W47M33   1989
641.5'77—dc20
89-21817
CIP

Reprinted in 1989

Sage Books/Swallow Press

Swallow Press / Ohio University Press
books are printed on acid-free paper. ∞

To my husband
WAITMAN W. McELFRESH

and to the memory of
our Mother and Dad

It will not detract from the above dedication
also to honor here all the old pioneer cowboys and
roundup cooks of the old west

INTRODUCTION

Wyoming today is a modern, progressive state, its people engaged in many and varied industries, including its first industry, livestock production.

This livestock industry, however, is more than a business in Wyoming; it is a way of life. The traditions which grew up on the great open range in the days of the big cattle trails from Texas have survived in today's modern cattle country with its mechanized operations. The rancher of 1960 may use an airplane to "go to town" or to hop East for a holiday, but he retains that Western neighborliness that characterized life on the plains around the turn of the century when neighbors were hundreds of miles apart.

One of the features of early day life in the West was the great annual roundup and the chuck wagon where food was cooked and served to the "hands." In recent years the chuck wagon has moved into more sophisticated settings; "chuck wagon feeds" appear at rodeo celebrations, at tourist entertainments and in private patios. The food at these affairs is frequently quite elaborate, but those who have eaten from the back end of a chuck wagon during a roundup say it's not up to the "real thing."

Of course, the chuck wagon is still used at some real roundups but old timers claim that the recipes and traditions of the early day roundup cooks are being forgotten, recipes of such cooks as Hi Pockets of the CY Ranch who could make honey of lima beans and who could stretch his menu to serve any number of visiting ranchers along with the cowpunchers on the roundup.

The author of this delightful "Chuck Wagon Cookbook" learned many of her recipes from Hi Pockets, and later on Mrs. McElfresh herself was a roundup cook for many years. Her book preserves for us the recipes and cooking methods of the Old West chuck wagon cooks.

The daughter of a noted Wyoming pioneer, Mary Hedgpeth Ash, Beth McElfresh is a true product of the West. The Hedgpeth family is mentioned in the Journal of John Udell written in 1859 and published in 1868. Joel Hedgpeth had moved in 1839 from Kentucky to Missouri where he became the first judge of his county; and a son Thomas R. Hedgpeth was a minister preaching over much of northwestern Missouri before the family moved on West. The Ash family were early ranchers in North Dakota and Montana before the coming of the Milwaukee railroad into those states.

Beth Ash was married in 1905 to W. W. McElfresh, a cowboy who had trailed herds up from Texas to Wyoming and nearby states. He was wagon boss for the famous CY holdings in South Dakota and for many years manager of their holdings in Wyoming. He later ran other spreads, including his own, and became widely known as "Scout," his wife as "Mrs. Scout."

In this book Mrs. McElfresh has included a few modern and traditional recipes given to her by members of her family and friends, but her chief endeavor has been to record the cooking methods and recipes of the cattle range as she learned them and used them serving meals off the end of a chuck wagon following the roundup. She even incorporates some of the cooking tips and health hints used on the range far from towns, railroads and doctors.

Joseph C. O'Mahoney
former United States Senator from Wyoming

CONTENTS

CHUCK WAGON FEED

If you wish to give a party out in the wide-open spaces; if you would like to serve what cowboys liked and were eating some fifty years ago, keep this in mind: Beans, beef, hot biscuits, and apple pie with hunks of longhorn cheese. If I were having a chuck wagon feed, that is what I would serve.

Hi Pockets baked lima beans, baked with good thick steak, cabbage cole slaw, hashed brown potatoes, sour dough biscuits, or sour milk soda biscuits, dried apple pie. Be sure to have a large bowl of sliced sweet onions. Don't forget to make a lot of boiled coffee. It is true that most cowboys drank coffee black, for they had no cream in the roundup. About the year 1905 cattle outfits began to furnish canned milk. Most of the boys poured in the canned milk until the coffee resembled a new saddle in color. You may add sugar, butter, and pickles to the menu.

SOUPS

SPLIT PEA SOUP

1 quart milk or canned milk
2 cups dried split peas

Cook peas until good and tender, mash peas, add milk, 1 tsp. butter. When good and hot (but don't boil) remove from stove. Add ½ tsp. garden sage and some black pepper. Serve with oyster crackers.

RED SALMON SOUP

1 can red salmon
1 tbsp. butter

1 quart milk
Black pepper to taste

Heat the milk, mash salmon and add to milk. Add butter and pepper. Serve with dry toast or crackers.

VEGETABLE SOUP

Have a good beef stock. Grind your vegetables and meat through a coarse grinder and add to the stock. Chop the onions (it makes them better to run them through the grinder), add salt and pepper. I find this makes a good vegetable soup.

CORN SOUP

To 1 quart of milk add 1 can of cream style corn. Add corn to hot milk. Then add 1 tbsp. butter and a little black pepper. Serve with crackers or cheese crackers.

TOMATO SOUP

1 can tomatoes (No. 2 can), ¼ tsp. soda. Heat tomatoes, add the soda, and allow to effervesce. Add 1 quart of boiling milk, 1 tbsp. butter, black pepper to taste. Serve with crackers or dry toast.

CHICKEN SOUP

Make a plain chicken soup. Thicken a little with a handful of white corn meal. Drop 1 egg into a pan of flour and rub until it crumbs, then drop the crumbs into the soup. Cook for a little bit; add pepper and salt. Serve with crackers.

POTATO SOUP

Cook and mash 4 large potatoes. Add 1 small chopped onion, 1 quart hot milk, salt, and 1 tbsp. butter. Before you remove from stove, add a bunch of chopped parsley. Serve with crackers or dry brown toast.

SALADS AND SALAD DRESSINGS

HOT CABBAGE AND BACON SLAW

Shred ½ head cabbage. Heat 1 cup salad dressing, thin with sour cream. Add cabbage. Let stand 3 minutes, low heat. Just before serving, add 6 slices bacon, broken. 6 servings.

PEPPER SALAD

Use one large green pepper, one large sweet onion sliced fine, 3 tomatoes peeled and diced into cubes. Salt a little. Put together with dressing made of ½ cup vinegar, ¼ cup water, 1 tsp. sugar, little black pepper, just a little paprika, 2 tbsp. salad oil. Mix and pour over salad.

TOMATO AND LETTUCE SALAD

Choose head of crisp lettuce, pull to pieces and leave in small chunks. Arrange in salad bowl; add 2 cups celery, diced quarters of 4 tomatoes that have been peeled. Add 2 green onions chopped fine. Pour over the center of the dish any dressing preferred. Garnish with 3 hard-cooked eggs that have been salted with celery salt.

CRUSHED PINEAPPLE SALAD

1 pkg. orange gelatin	1 small can crushed pineapple
1 cup hot water	1 small can white grapes
1 cup whipping cream	2 cups raw ground cranberries
1 cup sugar	

Pour 1 cup boiling water over orange gelatin. The cranberries and sugar are ground. After gelatin has cooled whip until light and frothy. Combine with 1 cup whipped cream. Add cranberries, pineapple, and grapes. Chill in mold.

HOT POTATO SALAD
(Even roundup cooks made potato salad)

6 potatoes	½ cup water
6 slices bacon	½ cup vinegar
½ cup onions	1 tsp. salt
1 tbsp. flour	1 tbsp. sugar

Boil medium sized potatoes in their jackets. Fry bacon very crisp. Remove from fat, crumble, and add to peeled cubed potatoes. Blend flour with bacon drippings in frying pan. Add water, salt, vinegar, and sugar. Cook until thick, pour over potatoes, chopped onions, and bacon. Mix well and serve hot.

WILTED LETTUCE
(An old-fashioned salad but very good)

Fry 4 slices cut-up bacon until crisp. Add and heat ¼ cup vinegar, 3 tbsp. water, 1 tbsp. sugar, 3 young green onions chopped fine, salt, and pepper. Add 2 quarts shredded leaf lettuce. Toss until wilted.

THANKSGIVING SALAD

2 cups cranberries	1 cup chopped walnut meats
2 cups sugar	1 pkg. lemon gelatin
2 oranges	¼ cup cold water
½ cup hot water	

Grind raw cranberries fine. Add sugar and let stand 10 minutes. Remove seeds and core from oranges and grind fine, including peel. Add orange and walnut meats to cranberry mixture. Soak gelatin in cold water for 5 minutes, then add hot water and stir until dissolved. Combine with fruit mixture. Pour into a mold. Chill until firm.

SAUERKRAUT SALAD

Combine 1 can (1 lb.) sauerkraut, well chilled and drained, 1 container (8 oz.) sour cream, 2 tsp. caraway seed, and 1 tsp. sugar. Toss lightly and serve.

BOILED SALAD DRESSING

Mix dry: 1 tbsp. flour, 3 tbsp. sugar, 1 tsp. mustard.

1 egg	½ cup vinegar
½ cup water	butter size of a walnut

Cook in the top of a double boiler over hot water until thick. When this is used for a fruit salad, add a little whipped sweet cream.

CARROT SALAD

1 cup grated raw carrot	1 cup chopped raw cabbage
1 cup chopped celery	

Combine 1 tbsp. lemon juice, ½ tsp. salt. Mix salad with a little boiled salad dressing.

COLE SLAW

¼ cup vinegar	3 eggs
½ tsp. salt	1 tbsp. butter
¼ tsp. black pepper	2 tbsp. cream
1 tbsp. sugar	3 cups cabbage

Heat in a double boiler the vinegar and seasonings (including the sugar and butter), bring to boiling heat. Beat eggs and add hot vinegar mixture to them very slowly. Cook until mixture thickens, then add cream. Remove the dressing from the fire and pour it while hot over the cabbage that has been chopped quite fine. Garnish with rings of hard-cooked eggs and serve when cold.

PICKLES AND KRAUT

3 quarts sliced cucumbers	1 tsp. cinnamon
1½ cups sliced onions	1 tsp. allspice
½ cup brown sugar	½ tsp. mustard
4 tsp. salt	1 tsp. tumeric
1 cup corn syrup	vinegar and water to cover

Slice cucumbers very thin, mix with onions and salt. Let soak over night, drain in the morning and put in a preserving kettle. Mix the spices with corn syrup and sugar and pour over the pickles, adding enough vinegar and a little water to cover. Bring to boiling point and boil 2 minutes. Pour into jars and seal.

DILL PICKLES

For ½ gallon, fill jar with medium sized cucumbers, then add heaping tbsp. salt, a medium sized bunch of dill, and fill jar with boiling water and seal. Set in the sun for a week or 10 days. Then the pickles are ready for use.

BEET AND CABBAGE RELISH

2 pints beets	¼ tsp. red pepper
2 pints cabbage	1 tsp. black pepper
½ cup horseradish	2 pints vinegar
2 cups brown sugar	

Boil the beets until tender, peel and put through food chopper with cabbage and horseradish. Mix them with vinegar, sugar, and pepper. Boil 10 minutes. Seal in glass jars.

KRAUT

Shred cabbage or cut with kraut cutter; pack lightly in quart glass jars; add 1 tsp. salt. Place silver knife inside jar. Fill with boiling water, seal, place in fairly warm place for 10 days, then store in fruit room. Mrs. Fred Miller of Sheridan, Wyo., adds 1 apple, chopped, to each jar.

GENERAL COOKERY

SWEET TABLE MUSTARD

(This is the Hi Pockets way of making table mustard, and the cowpunchers all loved it.)

Take 2 level tbsp. dry mustard, 2 level tsp. flour, 2 tbsp. sugar, 1 tsp. salt, 1 tsp. tumeric. Boil 3 tbsp. vinegar with 2 tbsp. water, add 1 tbsp. butter or salad oil. Pour over dry ingredients, mixing to a fairly thin paste. Hi Pockets used lard but perhaps salad oil or butter is better.

CORN BREAD POULTRY DRESSING

Make this dressing half cold corn bread and half white bread. Crumble the bread and add salt, sage and black pepper to suit taste. Add 1 lb. pork sausage. Pour warm water or chicken broth over the bread. Add 1 small onion chopped fine, with 3 sticks celery. Mix well, then fry in a pan on top of stove with a little butter. If it gets too dry, add a little water. Fry on stove 20 minutes. Cool, and stuff chicken or turkey.

SCALLOPED POTATOES AND CARROTS

(This dish I learned to make from an old time ranch cook.)

Pare and slice thin 3 cups potatoes. Scrape and slice 3 cups carrots. In a buttered baking dish put half the potatoes and carrots. Put in some butter, flour, and salt. Prepare the other layers in the same manner until all the ingredients are used. Pour 2 cups milk over the whole. Bake 400° 60 minutes. For this dish, use 4 tbsp. butter, 4 tbsp. flour, 2 tsp. salt, 2 cups rich milk.

SALT PORK WITH GRAVY

(Many years ago, my husband and I met an old stage driver at Elk Mountain, Wyo. He said he was driving stage and riding Pony Express at the same time Bill Cody was. This old stage driver was batching in a little log cabin at the foot of Elk Mountain. He gave me this recipe. It makes a good meal when on a camping trip.)

1¼ lbs. salt pork
2   tbsp. flour
a little salt and pepper

¾ cup corn meal
2 cups canned milk

Have salt pork cut in slices ¼ inch thick. Cover with hot water for a few minutes, then drain and dip each piece in corn meal and brown slowly in fat in skillet. Drain off all but two tbsp. of fat, mix in flour. Brown for two minutes, stirring well; then add milk and cook for five minutes. Add salt and pepper. Serve with slices of sweet onions and potatoes cooked in their jackets.

ONE DISH MEAL:
CABBAGE MEAT ROLLS

2 cups uncooked rice
1 cup chopped celery
1 tsp. salt
1 beaten egg

1 lb. good hamburger
2 chopped green peppers
7 or 8 cabbage leaves
1 tbsp. catsup

Mix all ingredients together and mix well. Make into 7 or 8 balls, wrapping each ball in a cabbage leaf. Place a small layer of shredded cabbage in bottom of baking dish. Put in the cabbage rolls, then a small layer of shredded cabbage on top. Add 1¼ cups water and bake in a slow oven for 2 hours. Serve with corn meal rolls, and lots of butter.

(Try molasses pie for dessert with this dish.)

CORN MEAL ROLLS

1½ cups flour
2 tbsp. melted shortening
½ tsp. soda
1 tbsp. sugar
½ tsp. salt

¾ cup yellow corn meal
1 egg
2 tsp. baking powder
½ cup sour milk

Sift together flour, sugar, salt, and baking powder. Add corn meal, combine with the beaten egg, melted shortening, and sour milk. Roll ½ inch thick. Cut as for cookies; brush tops with melted butter. Fold over half and bake in hot oven.

ONE DISH MEAL: HI POCKETS'
BAKED LIMA BEANS WITH STEAK

(Hi Pockets had a way with meat! This one dish recipe is especially good.)

Soak 2 cups lima beans over night. Simmer beans until nearly done. Use dutch oven or large casserole to cook this in:

2 lbs. round steak
1 tsp. salt
few grains pepper

½ tsp. dry mustard
1 tbsp. brown sugar

Tenderize steak by pounding, cut into 4 pieces. Roll steak in flour. Put layer of beans, then layer of the steak, then layer of beans. Repeat until casserole is nearly full of steak and beans. Mix remaining dry ingredients with 1 cup tomato juice and 1 tbsp. bacon fat. Pour mixture over beans and meat. Place an onion on top and bake until meat is tender and beans are done. Add a little water from time to time if mixture becomes too dry.

SCRAPPLE

Cowboys loved the way the old-time roundup cooks made scrapple. Boil 3 lbs. beef. Get a cheap cut well down on the leg; have a little fat on the piece of meat. Boil until very tender. Run the meat through the food chopper. Put the meat back into the broth and bring to a boil; thicken with corn meal until you have a thick mush. Pour into a deep pan. When cold, slice, roll in corn meal, and fry in meat fryings. Serve with scrambled eggs that little green onions have been cut up in.

COW PUNCHER STEW

(This is a stew Hi Pockets made early in the spring before range cattle were fat and ready to butcher.)

2 lbs. lean bacon	carrots
onions	cabbage
potatoes	turnips

Cut bacon in small squares and boil until about half done. Then add chopped vegetables. Season to taste. When almost done put in a few Leather Apron Dumplings.

STEAKS

I have never found anyone who could cook meats as well as the old roundup cooks. I'm going to tell you how Hi Pockets cooked his steak:

chicken-fry

When you chicken-fry a steak, do not use lard. Cut extra fat and tallow from steak or other piece of beef. Fry out in heavy iron frying pan. Leave these cracklings in pan along with drippings when frying steak. Tenderize steak, salt, pepper, and roll in flour; put into pan of smoking hot fat.

pan broil

To pan broil a rare steak, tenderize steak and cut into serving size pieces. Have a heavy iron frying pan hot (I like best the dutch oven type). Sprinkle a little salt into the frying pan. Now put in steak, salt and pepper lightly. Turn once every minute until done to suit taste. Serve on hot plate with butter dotted on top. (A very little tallow may be used instead of the salt in the skillet.)

COWPUNCHER CHILI PIE

1 lb. ground beef	1 large onion
1 cup chili beans, cooked	¼ tsp. chili powder
1 tbsp. drippings	1 tsp. salt
1 cup tomatoes	1 tsp. worcestershire sauce

Melt drippings in frying pan. Add crumbled ground meat and chopped onion. Fry together until partly done. Add seasonings, cooked beans, and tomatoes. Simmer for 15 minutes. Pour into deep baking dish and top with corn bread batter. Bake 20 minutes at 425°.

CORN BREAD BATTER

½ cup flour	¾ cup corn meal
2 tsp. baking powder	1 tbsp. sugar
1 beaten egg	½ cup milk
2 tbsp. melted shortening	

Mix well and pour over chili pie.

LEATHER APRONS
(When Hi Pockets taught me to make these dumplings he said, "This recipe came from the South with me, and many a cowpuncher trailing cattle up over the Chisholm Trail has enjoyed my Leather Aprons.)

2 cups flour   ½ tsp. salt
cold water

Sift flour and salt, add water to make stiff dough. Roll paper thin.
Cut into squares. Drop into boiling beef broth. Cook 12 minutes.
(These dumplings are good in chicken broth or beans that are quite
soupy. The secret of making them is to roll them very thin.)

VINEGAR DROP DUMPLINGS
*(Here is something old-time ranch cooks made often. It makes a
lovely dessert served with good cream.)*

To 1 pint of hot water and ½ cup vinegar, add $^2/_3$ cup sugar, 1 tbsp.
butter, 1 tsp. nutmeg. Put the above on the stove to boil. Then
drop in the dumplings. Place a tight lid on the pan and boil ten
minutes.

to make the dumplings:

1 egg, ¼ tsp. salt, $^1/_3$ cup milk, 1 tbsp. sugar, 1 heaping tsp. good
baking powder: add flour and mix well to a very stiff batter. Drop
by spoonsful into the boiling water and vinegar. This will make 6
helpings.

EGG NOODLES
Beat 2 eggs lightly, add 1 tbsp. heavy cream to each egg. Add pinch
of salt, and flour to make a very stiff dough. Roll very thin, dredge
with flour to keep from sticking. Roll into tight roll, then slice in
thin strips. Drop in boiling soup. Boil 10 minutes.

EARLY DAY BEANS

3 cups red beans	salt to taste
¾ cup brown sugar	4 tbsp. butter
¼ cup lemon juice	1 tsp. mustard

Soak beans overnight. Add salt and cook slowly until tender, adding more water if necessary. Add sugar, butter, and lemon juice. Serve with hot rolls or corn bread.

BAKED BEANS

Soak 2 cups navy beans overnight in enough water to cover. Next morning cook on top of stove for 20 minutes. Pour beans into a bean pot, add 1 can of tomatoes rubbed through a colander, ¼ cup brown sugar, ½ tsp. ginger, ½ tsp. mustard, ½ tsp. black pepper, ¼ tsp. salt, 1 tbsp. dark molasses. The molasses gives a good brown color to the beans. Last of all, add 4 strips of bacon over the top of the beans. Bake 3 hours.

SOUR DOUGH PANCAKES

for sour dough batter

Use gallon container, either glass or crockery. 2 qts. water; add enough flour to make thick batter. To this batter add ½ yeast cake and 1 large, raw potato, peeled and quartered, and 1 tbsp. sugar. Let this mixture set in a warm place for a few days until quite sour.

for pancakes

1 cup sour dough batter	1 tbsp. lard
1 cup flour	½ tsp. soda
1 tsp. sugar	½ tsp. salt

Add enough water to the ingredients to make batter for pancakes. (Note: always mix flour and water batter and add to the sour dough batter to make up for that used in baking.)

POTATO PANCAKES

(Fifty years ago roundup cooks did not have many eggs with which to cook. Sometimes Hi Pockets managed to trade some beef to a ranch woman for eggs and milk. Then he gave the cowpunchers a treat. Potato pancakes were one of the treats.)

2 cups grated potatoes	milk
1 egg	salt
3 tbsp. flour	1 small onion, grated

Pare and grate potatoes into cold water to keep them from discoloring. Drain well and add well-beaten egg, flour, salt, and onion, and enough milk to make a stiff batter. Cook in frying pan with hot fat ½ inch deep. A large spoonful of batter makes a good-sized cake. Cook until crisp and brown. Drain on brown paper and serve with syrup.

WELSH RABBIT

1 tbsp. butter	1 cup milk
1 tbsp. flour	pinch of salt
¼ tsp. mustard	a little black pepper
1 lb. sharp cheese	

Shave or grate the cheese. Make a white sauce in the top of a double boiler, of all ingredients except the cheese. Mix and cook for a few minutes, add cheese, cook and stir until it is melted. Serve on hot toasted bread or crackers.

WELSH RABBIT

1 tbsp. butter	¼ tsp. mustard
1 tbsp. flour	¼ to 1 lb. cheese, according to richness desired. Shave or grate cheese.
1 cup milk	
½ tsp. salt	
few grains black pepper	

Make white sauce in top of double boiler, using all the ingredients except the cheese and mixing the mustard with the other dry ingredients. Set the top part of the boiler over hot but not boiling water. Add the cheese, cook and stir until it is melted. Add 2 beaten eggs just after cheese has melted. Cook until eggs have thickened mixture. Serve on crackers or toast. (Rabbit is fine served with old style lager beer as a beverage.)

CHICKEN AND SPAGHETTI

1 fryer, 2 to 3 lbs.
1 small can tomato paste
2 cloves chopped garlic
1 tsp. cinnamon
½ tsp. mixed spices
  (no peppers)
salt and pepper

1 medium onion, chopped
  fine
1 cube butter
3½ cups water
1 cup grated cheese (Kaseri, Romano, or Kefaloteri)

Cut chicken into serving pieces and wash thoroughly. Thin out tomato paste with 2 cups water. Brown chicken slightly in ½ cube butter, for about 10 minutes. Transfer to saucepan. In skillet add remaining butter and saute onion for 3 minutes. Add tomato paste and simmer 2 minutes. Pour over chicken. Add cinnamon, garlic, and 1 cup water to cover. More or less water may be needed. Salt and pepper to taste. Reduce heat to medium and cover. Cook for 45 minutes or until chicken is tender. Stir occasionally, being careful not to break chicken. Serve chicken on large platter.

Cook spaghetti in boiling water which has been salted, and drain thoroughly. Brown ½ cube butter slightly in saucepan over high flame and pour over spaghetti; mix thoroughly, alternating with part of sauce from chicken and grated cheese. Top with the remaining sauce and cheese. More cheese may be added at the table if anyone desires it.

BREADS AND CAKES

SOUR MILK BISCUITS

2 cups flour
2 tsp. baking powder
2 tbsp. lard

1 tsp. salt
¼ tsp. soda
1 cup sour milk

Sift dry ingredients into mixing bowl. Rub in lard with finger tips. Add sour milk. Mix into a soft and spongy dough. Roll ½ inch thick and cut. Lightly flour shallow pan or cookie sheet, place biscuits not too close together, and bake 12 minutes.

SPOON BREAD

(This bread was much loved by old time cowpunchers from Texas. The chuckwagon cooks baked it in the heavy dutch ovens.)

1 cup yellow or white corn
  meal
1 heaping tbsp. butter
yolks of 3 eggs, beaten

1 tsp. baking powder
½ tsp. salt
1½ cups canned milk

Mix the corn meal, butter, and a little bit of boiling water to dissolve and make smooth. Let cool. Add egg yolks, well beaten, then the baking powder. The milk should be scalded slightly, but do not boil. Then add the stiffly beaten egg whites. The batter will be thin. Pour into a well-greased baking dish 2 inches deep. Bake 30 minutes at 425°. The spoon bread will be soft inside, brown outside. Dip out in large tablespoonsful.

BOSTON BROWN BREAD

1 cup corn meal
1 cup rye flour
1 cup graham flour
1 tsp. soda
4 tsp. baking powder

1 tsp. salt
¾ cup molasses
2 cups sour milk
2 cups sweet milk

Mix the dry ingredients and add the molasses and the milk. Beat the mixture thoroughly, and pour into greased molds until they are about ¾ full. Cover loosely to keep out the moisture, and steam for 3½ hours. Remove the covers and bake the bread in oven for 10 minutes to dry off.

NUT BREAD

3½ cups flour
4 tsp. baking powder
1 cup sugar
1 tsp. salt

1 cup sweet milk
2 cups nuts, chopped
4 tbsp. melted fat
1 egg

Combine all ingredients and stir well. Pour in bake pans and let stand for 15 minutes. Bake at 375° for 45 minutes.

CORN MEAL BREAD

(This is especially good with fried chicken and chicken gravy.)

2 cups corn meal mixed with 2 cups boiling water. Add beaten yolks of 3 eggs, 1½ cups milk, 4 tbsp. melted butter, 4 tsp. baking powder, 1 tsp. salt. Fold in the stiffly beaten whites of 3 eggs. Pour into a well-greased, heated casserole and bake 30 minutes in a moderate oven. Serve with lots of butter or chicken gravy.

SUET BREAD

(A nifty German breakfast. An old time German recipe brought to this country from Germany by Margaret Shenefelt's great-grandmother, who in turn brought it from Iowa to Wyoming, handing it down to her children.)

4 cups suet
7 cups flour

4 tsp. salt
1 tsp. pepper

Chop suet and remove fibers. Add flour, salt, and pepper and mix like pie crust. Put in sack and boil in large kettle of water. Put saucer or jar top in bottom of kettle to keep sack from sticking. Boil about 4 hours, adding more water from time to time as it is needed. Turn out on platter to cool. Keep in refrigerator. As needed, slice and heat on pie plate; when light brown serve very hot with coffee.

JONNY CAKE OR CORN BREAD

1¼ cups sweet milk	1 egg
2 tbsp. sugar	1 tsp. salt
2 tbsp. melted butter	1 cup flour
1 cup corn meal	2 tsp. baking powder

Mix well and pour batter into pan in which the butter was melted (melt butter in 8 × 12 inch cake pan), and bake until brown. By adding a little more milk, one can use this recipe for corn meal pancakes to be baked on a griddle.

CHUCK WAGON BREAD
(Hi Pockets made SOUR DOUGH BREAD according to the recipe upon page 24.)

SOUR DOUGH BISCUITS

2 cups flour	1 tsp. salt
½ tsp. soda	1 tsp. baking powder
2 tbsp. melted lard	1 tsp. sugar

Sift dry ingredients into bowl. Make hole in flour and into this pour enough sour dough mixture, plus the melted shortening, to make medium stiff dough. Shape into small rolls. Set in warm place to rise until light. Bake as you would light rolls.
(Sour Dough Batter recipe on page 24.)

WHITE BREAD OR ROLLS

2 cups milk
2 tbsp. sugar
1 tbsp. salt

1 cake yeast
2 tbsp. melted shortening

Scald milk, add salt, sugar, and shortening. Let cool. Dissolve yeast cake in ½ cup warm water and 1 tsp. sugar. Mix with flour to make a stiff dough. Knead dough quickly and lightly until smooth and elastic. Let rise in a warm place. This will make 1 loaf and a pan of rolls.

CUSH

(The dish called "cush" was much used by old time chuck wagon cooks when trailing cattle up from the South. The recipe was given to me by my Aunt Ruth Campbell, whose husband brought the recipe to her when he came back from Lee's Confederate Army.)

Crumble left-over corn bread in a heavy iron frying pan. Season well with drippings from meat fryings, add a little water, salt and black pepper to taste. Let cook until crusty, stirring often. Serve with good meat or chicken gravy.

CORN PONE

Mix 1 cup yellow corn meal, ½ tsp. salt, 1 tbsp. sugar, and cold water to make a thick dough as wet as can be shaped into biscuit-size cakes. Bake on a greased pan in a hot oven at 450° until brown. This will crumble but has a wonderful flavor. Serve with black-eye peas (see next paragraph).

(Soak peas overnight, then boil until tender; season with salt and pepper. Boil peas with ham bone or a piece of bacon. Keep adding water while the peas are cooking, so that there will be lots of pot likker to eat with the corn pone.)

RANCH TOAST

Make a batter with ½ cup sour milk, 1 egg, a little salt, ½ tsp. soda, small spoon of sugar; add flour to make a thin batter. Dip each slice of medium dry bread in the batter, fry in cast iron skillet in hot lard or frying fats. This is good with ham and maple syrup.

CINNAMON TOAST

Toast the bread brown; mix a little sugar, butter, and cinnamon together, spread the mixture on toast. Toast in the broiler a little bit more. Serve with fruit.

EGG TOAST

Two eggs well beaten; add a little salt and 2 tbsp. cream. Beat well. Dip medium dry bread in egg and fry in brown fat. Serve with crisp bacon.

HAM TOAST

Chop some lean boiled ham fine. Put it into a pan with a little pepper and a lump of butter. When quite hot, stir in 2 well-beaten eggs mixed with 1 tbsp. of cream. Mix well and spread on hot buttered toast.

(NOTE: Sausage and eggs scrambled together is good on toast. For this use Ranch Toast.)

SANDWICHES

Baked Bean Sandwich

Mash 2 cups baked beans with 1 tsp. sweet mustard (see Index for Hi Pockets recipe), 2 slices of sweet onion, chopped fine; add 1 tbsp. sharp salad dressing. Use one slice of dark bread and one of white bread. To make the sandwich, butter one slice of bread and put the sandwich together with a crisp lettuce leaf.

Cucumber and Tomato Sandwich

Slice cucumbers and tomatoes quite thin. Spread with mayonnaise dressing to which some crumbled crisp fried bacon has been added.

SALLY GOODEN

(This easy coffee cake is something roundup cooks and ranch wives have been making for the last 50 years when company drops in and something has to be made quickly.)

1 egg	½ cup sugar
½ cup milk	4 tbsp. shortening
1 good cup bread flour	3 tsp. baking powder
½ tsp. salt	

- - - - - -

2 tbsp. brown sugar	½ tsp. cinnamon

Mix first 7 ingredients together; mix well but do not beat. Bake 20 minutes in an 8-inch pan. Sprinkle the top with brown sugar and cinnamon before you put the cake in the oven. Bake at 375°. Serve with a cup of coffee or tea.

GINGER CREAMS

(All cowpunchers and ranchhands liked ginger creams.)

½ cup shortening	1 cup sugar
1 egg	1 cup molasses
4 cups flour	½ tsp. salt
1 tsp. nutmeg	2 tsp. ginger
1 tsp. cloves	1 tsp. cinnamon
1 cup hot water	2 tsp. soda

Cream shortening and sugar. Add egg, molasses, and hot water to which soda has been added. Sift the remaining dry ingredients together and add to the liquid mixture. Drop by teaspoonsful on oiled cookie sheet. Bake until brown.

SCOTCH SHORT BREAD
(A dessert. Serve with coffee or tea.)

3½ cups sifted flour	½ cup sugar
1 cup butter	¼ tsp. salt

Sift the flour, salt, and sugar on a bread board. Break butter into small pieces and work into the dry ingredients by pressing with the palm of the hand and the wrist until there is a smooth, even mixture. Make the dough into a ball and roll out about ¾ of an inch thick. Place in a pan with high sides to prevent the short bread from browning too quickly around the edges, and prick the surface with a fork. Bake in a very moderate oven, 300°, for 35 minutes. Allow the short bread to stand an hour or two before serving so that it becomes crisp and thoroughly set, then break bread into pieces.

DOUGHNUTS
(These are very good.)

1 cup sugar	1 cup sour milk
3 tsp. fat	2 eggs
1 tsp. soda	½ tsp. cinnamon
4 cups flour	

Flour enough to roll. After cutting, let rise 30 minutes before dropping in hot fat.

ROUNDUP DOUGHNUTS

2 eggs
1 cup sour dough batter
½ cup sour milk, into which
   1 scant tsp. soda has been
   dissolved

1 cup sugar
1 tbsp. melted lard
little nutmeg
pinch salt
1 tsp. baking powder

Flour enough to roll. After cutting, let rise 30 minutes before dropping in hot fat.

BURNT SUGAR ANGEL FOOD CAKE
(For one living on a ranch with many fresh eggs, this cake is a delicious one to make.)

1 pint flour, 1 $\frac{1}{3}$ pint sugar; sift 6 times together. 15 egg whites, ¼ tsp. salt. Beat until when bowl is turned upside down egg whites will not slide. When partly beaten, add 1 level tsp. cream tartar. Finish beating. Add 1 tsp. vanilla, 2 tbsp. burnt sugar. Stir flour and sugar in very slowly. Bake in ungreased pan 1¼ hours in a very slow oven. Add a little burnt sugar to the icing.

BAKELESS CAKE

Use ½ cup butter, 1 cup sugar, 1 egg yolk, 1 large can pineapple (crushed), 1 cup nuts, chopped, 3 tbsp. cream, 1 package vanilla wafers. Put a layer of vanilla wafers in a shallow pan. Mix ingredients together. Spread layer of filling on wafers. Do this until 3 layers of wafers and 2 of filling are completed. Set to cool 4 hours. Serve with whipped cream.

HI POCKETS' SPICE CAKE

1   cup sugar
½   cup butter
1   tsp. soda
½   tsp. cinnamon
1½ cups flour

1 cup sour milk
1 egg
1 tsp. nutmeg
pinch of salt
(cream sugar and butter)

Dissolve soda in sour milk; mix well with sugar and butter. Add egg, nutmeg, cinnamon, salt, and flour. Frost with 7-Minute icing.

WHITE BIRTHDAY CAKE

2 cups sugar
2 cups milk
3 cups flour
4 egg whites

$^2/_3$ cups butter
1 tsp. orange extract
2 heaping tsp. baking powder

Beat whites of eggs, sugar, and butter together until very light, then add half the milk, 1 cup of flour with the baking powder. Stir until smooth, then add the rest of the milk, stir until smooth; then add the rest of the flour. Flavor. Bake in layers. Put together with orange butter.

ORANGE BUTTER

2 tbsp. butter
3 tbsp. milk
1 tsp. orange extract

2 cups powdered sugar
¼ tsp. grated orange rind
few drops lemon extract

Work until nice and smooth; add milk a little at a time until of right consistency to spread.

LAZY WOMAN'S CAKE

2   eggs
½   tsp. salt
1½ cups flour

1 cup sugar
1 tsp. flavoring
2 tsp. baking powder

Beat together the eggs, sugar, salt, flavoring. Sift together the flour and baking powder and add to mixture. Bring to a boil ½ cup milk with 3 tbsp. butter; add hot butter and milk to the above mixture a little at a time. Beat well. Bake in a loaf or 2 layers at about 375° or 400°.

ROUNDUP FRUIT CAKE

1½	cups sugar	½	cup butter or lard
1	tsp. soda	1	tsp. baking powder
1	tbsp. black molasses	1	cup applesauce
1	tsp. cinnamon	1	tsp. cloves
1	cup raisins	1	cup chopped figs
1	cup chopped nuts	2¾	cups flour
	(if desired)		

Bake in moderate oven with brown paper over the loaf pan. This is a good cheap fruit cake.

HI POCKETS' POOR MAN CAKE

1	cup sugar	½	cup lard
1	cup water	½	cup chopped walnuts
	pinch of salt	1	tsp. allspice

Put the above in a pan and boil 4 minutes. Let cook, then add 2 cups flour and 1 tsp. soda that have been sifted together. Bake in moderate oven until firm.

CRUMB CAKE
(A favorite cake)

Mix like pie crust 2 cups flour, 2 tsp. baking powder, 1½ cups sugar, ¾ cup butter. Save a small cupful for top. To remaining add ¾ cup milk, 2 eggs, flavoring. Beat until creamy. Spread in shallow pan and cover with the small cupful of crumbs. Bake at 375° until nice and brown.

DARK CRUMB CAKE

Mix 1 cup white sugar, 1 cup brown sugar, 2 cups flour, ½ cup lard. Save ½ cup of the crumbly mixture for top. To remaining add 2 eggs, 1 cup sour milk, 1 tsp. soda. Pour into shallow pan and cover with the crumbs. For variety, nut meats may be sprinkled over top before baking.

BURNT SUGAR CAKE

½ cup butter	½ cup sugar
1 cup water	2 cups flour
yolks of 2 eggs	

To above add 4 tsp. burnt sugar, 1 tsp. vanilla, ½ cup flour. Beat 5 minutes, then add 2 tsp. baking powder and whites of eggs beaten stiff. Bake at 375°. Ice with 7-Minute icing.

(NOTE: The following two fine recipes were given to me by a Greek friend, Mrs. Bessie Juroszek, of Sheridan, Wyoming. Of the first, Mrs. Juroszek says, "This dish of chicken and spaghetti was handed down from my grandmother to my mother, then to me. It makes a very tasty and delicious dish which is quite filling." The Walnut Honey Cake is a Greek pastry found in many Greek homes today. It is not necessarily a dessert but is usually reserved only for guests and special occasions. Because of the richness of the pastry, it is served with coffee or just a glass of water.)

WALNUT HONEY CAKE
(Karidopita)

1 lb. shelled walnuts (ground finely)
1 tsp. each of cinnamon, cloves, and nutmeg
12 slices Zweiback
1 lb. powdered sugar
1 cube butter
12 eggs

Beat egg yolks. Add powdered sugar slowly and beat well. Then add nuts and crumbled zwieback and mix well. Next add spices and beat thoroughly. Fold in beaten egg whites. Spread batter in pan and add butter. Bake 25-30 minutes in oven 375°. While still warm, pour syrup over cake, and let soak in. (See recipe for syrup below.) Cut cake in small squares and serve.

SYRUP

1½ cups honey
1½ cups water
1 cup sugar

Boil sugar and water for thin syrup about 2 to 4 minutes. Then add honey. Cool then pour slowly over cake. If a less sweeter syrup is desired, use less honey and more water.

WAFFLES
(May be made with white or whole wheat flour.)

2 cups flour
½ tsp. salt
2 rounded tsp. good baking powder
1 tbsp. cooking corn starch

1½ cups milk
¼ cup salad oil
1 tsp. sugar
2 eggs, well beaten

Mix well, then bake. (Especially wonderful with good whole wheat flour.)

CAKE FILLINGS, ICINGS

QUICK ICING

Make a quick icing for an 8 or 9 inch square or circular plain white cake by melting 2 or 3 tbsp. butter or margarine in a skillet and adding $1/3$ cup brown sugar. Mix well over low heat, then add a cup of shredded coconut spread over the surface of the cake; toast carefully in broiler.

COFFEE BUTTER FROSTING

¼   cup butter
1½ cups confectioner's sugar

1½-2 tbsp. strong coffee
½ tsp. vanilla

Cream butter until very light. Sift and gradually add sugar, working it in thoroughly. Moisten with coffee, adding only a teaspoon at a time. Finally add vanilla and spread on cake.

7-MINUTE ICING

Mix 1 egg white, ¾ cup sugar, 3 tbsp. hot water, 3 tbsp. white corn syrup, ¼ tsp. cream of tartar, and a pinch of salt. In top of double boiler, place over boiling water and beat all the time icing is cooking. Cook until mixture is thick enough to stand in peaks. Remove from heat. Add a few drops of peppermint.

CREAM FILLING

1 tbsp. corn starch
1 cup milk
1 egg yolk
⅛ tsp. salt

1 tsp. vanilla
2 tbsp. confectioner's sugar
1 tsp. butter

Mix the corn starch with 2 tbsp. milk. Heat the rest of the milk in a double boiler and stir the corn starch part slowly into it. Stir the mixture until it is smooth and cook it for 15 minutes. Add the beaten egg yolk and cook 2 minutes longer. Remove from the fire and add the salt, sugar, and butter. Beat well. Add flavor. Cool before spreading on layers.

CHOCOLATE FILLING

yolks 2 eggs
1½ cups sugar
½ cup milk

4 squares chocolate
2 tsp. vanilla
few grains salt

Melt chocolate. Beat egg yolks very light. Add sugar and salt, continue beating. Add milk and butter. Cook over flame until it boils, stirring all the time. When it has boiled for one minute, take from fire and add melted chocolate and vanilla. Beat until thick enough to spead and holds its shape.

PIES

MOLASSES PIE

2 cups molasses	½ cup sugar
½ cup water	5 eggs
pinch of salt	1 tsp. cooking corn starch
pinch of soda	1 tsp. butter
dash of nutmeg	

Sorghum is the best molasses for this pie. Save the whites of 2 eggs for top of pie. Beat the 3 eggs and 2 yolks, add 2 cups of molasses, sugar, water, salt. Pour into top of double boiler, add corn starch; then place over hot water and stir while cooking. Cook until quite thick. Stir in soda, butter, nutmeg. Set aside to cool while baking one-crust pie shell; bake on outside of pie pan so that it won't shrink. When the filling is cool, pour into pie shell. Make meringue and pile on top of pie; place in oven until light brown. This makes a large pie.

PIE CRUST

1½ cups flour	¼ tsp. baking powder
½ tsp. salt	$^1/_3$ cup lard

Rub lard into flour into which salt and baking powder have been mixed. Add enough cold water to make a very stiff dough. Roll thin. Line pie tin and stick all over with fork. Bake a pale brown and use for lemon and cream pie. This makes two shells or one 2-crust pie.

COWPUNCHER'S DRIED APPLE PIE

2 cups cooked dried apples	1 tbsp. butter
1 cup cooked raisins	1 tbsp. vinegar
¾ cup brown sugar	1 tsp. cinnamon

In place of vinegar, you may use 2 tbsp. of lemon juice with the grated rind of one small orange.

MOLASSES PIE

(Molasses pie and molasses butter are two recipes that have been handed down in my mother's family for more than a hundred years. They came from Kentucky to Missouri in 1838 by oxen teams with my great-grandmother, Jane Hedgpeth. Then in 1858 the recipes went with her to California by oxen and by camels, as the government sent out camels to help the pioneers cross the desert.)

¾ cup sugar
½ cup butter
½ cup molasses
½ tsp. soda

2 eggs
¼ cup boiling water
1½ cups flour

Mix sugar, flour, and butter together. Save out ½ cup of this mixture to be used on top of the pie. Beat the eggs and add the molasses and boiling water into which the soda has been dissolved; add to sugar mixture. Pour into a large unbaked pastry shell. Sprinkle the crumb mixture over top of pie. Bake at 375° for 40 minutes. Serve with whipped cream. This may be baked without a pastry shell. (100% pure sorghum is best for this pie.)

MOLASSES BUTTER

1 cup molasses
pinch of salt
2 eggs

2 tbsp. butter
dash of nutmeg
pinch of soda

Bring to a boil in a double boiler all the ingredients except the eggs. Then add the well beaten eggs, and cook until thick. (100% pure sorghum is best for this butter. Small children like this butter as a spread on bread.)

APPLE DENVER PIE

(When my husband was brand inspector for Wyoming and Nebraska, we lived in Denver, Colorado. My landlady was famous for the apple pies she baked. She gave me this recipe.)

6 tart apples
2 tbsp. butter
2 cups water
½ cup brown sugar

1 tbsp. flour
1 tsp. nutmeg
1 cup white sugar

Wash, peel, and core apples; place cores and peelings in saucepan with 2 cups of water and boil down until one cup of juice is left. Strain; add to this juice the sugar, flour, nutmeg, and butter. Place saucepan on stove and boil until it is a little thick, then cool. Line a pie pan with a rich pie crust. Slice apples into crust; then pour the thickened juice over apples; place top crust on. Dampen pie with a little cold water and sprinkle with a little white sugar. Bake at 240° until apples are done and pie nice and brown.

ORANGE PIE

1½ cups strained orange juice
  (sweetened)
3 eggs

2 tbsp. corn starch
1 tbsp. butter
grated rind of 1 orange

Using only egg yolks with other ingredients cook until thick in top of double boiler. Cool and pour into baked pie shell. Use egg whites for the meringue.

MERINGUE

Beat egg whites until quite stiff. Add 3 tbsp. powdered sugar. Pile on top of pie and brown in oven.

HI POCKETS' BUTTERSCOTCH PIE

1 cup brown sugar
2 large tbsp. flour

1 cup water
1 tbsp. butter

Cook in double boiler 8 minutes, then add 1 cup of milk and beaten yolks of 2 eggs. Cook until thick. Pour into baked crust. Beat whites for meringue.

(This pie is good, but cheap to make.)

BURNT SUGAR PIE

2 cups hot milk. Add to the milk 2 tbsp. burnt sugar. Add 1 cup sugar, 1 tsp. butter, 3 egg yolks well beaten, 1 tsp. vanilla. Beat all together and cook in top of double boiler until thick. Cool, then spoon into baked pie crust. Beat whites for meringue for top of pie. Make meringue same as for rhubarb pie.

BURNT SUGAR PUDDING

To make the pudding, use the recipe above for burnt sugar pie. Serve pudding with whipped cream.

CREAM PIE
(Hi Pockets called this his Christmas Cream Pie.)

$1/3$	cup sugar	$1/3$	cup flour
$1/4$	tsp. salt	1	tall can milk
2	eggs	1	tsp. vanilla or almond
1	9-inch baked pie shell		extract
$1 1/2$	cup peaches (canned)		

Mix sugar, flour, and salt, slowly add milk. Cook in double boiler until thick, stirring constantly. Add small amount of hot mixture to slightly beaten eggs; now stir egg mixture into hot cream mixture. Cool. Add extract. Spread 1 cup sliced peaches in bottom of pie shell, pour custard over top. Arrange remaining peach slices on top. Serve with whipped cream if desired.

SOUR CREAM RAISIN PIE

1 cup sour cream
1 scant cup sugar
¼ tsp. cloves
3 egg yolks and 1 white

²/₃ cup raisins
½ tsp. cinnamon
1 tsp. salt

Put cream and raisins together over slow fire. Beat 3 egg yolks and 1 white. Add sugar, spice, salt; beat well. Add to the cream and raisins and cook, stirring constantly, as it burns easily. Pour into a baked pie shell. Cover with a meringue made with 2 egg whites. When pie has cooled, brown in the oven to a light brown.

RHUBARB PIE

Pour boiling water over 2½ cups rhubarb that has been cut into small pieces. Let stand 5 minutes and drain. Add 1 cup sugar, 1 tbsp. butter, 2 tbsp. flour, 3 tbsp. water, yolks of 2 eggs. Bake in one crust, use extra egg whites for meringue.

MERINGUE

2 egg whites
4 tbsp. sugar
1 tsp. vanilla

pinch of salt
1 tbsp. cold water
½ tsp. almond extract

Add salt and egg whites and water; beat until stiff, fold in the sugar, add flavoring, and pile on top of pie in little peaks. Place in oven at 300° until light brown.

MOCK LEMON PIE

(Were you ever way out in the wide open spaces with a yen for a lemon pie, and the nearest lemon forty miles away, and only a horse for transportation?)

1 cup sugar	1½	cups water
3 tbsp. flour	2	tbsp. strong vinegar
1 egg and yolks 2 eggs	1	tsp. lemon flavoring

Beat egg and 2 yolks together; add sugar, water, vinegar, and flavoring. Cook in double boiler until thick. Use 2 beaten egg whites with pinch of salt and 2 tsp. sugar for meringue for pie. Brown in oven.

SODA CRACKER PIE

3 egg whites	1	cup sugar
16 soda crackers	¼	tsp. baking powder
½ cup nut meats	1	tsp. vanilla

Beat egg whites until stiff. Add 1 cup sugar gradually, then add the soda crackers which have been rolled fine, and combine with the baking powder. Last, add nut meats and vanilla. Spread in buttered 9-inch pie plate and bake 325° oven for 30 minutes. When cold cover with a layer of fresh strawberries or bananas. Top with sweetened whipped cream. Chill 2 hours before serving.

FRIED PIES

(Hi Pockets made this often. He fried them in a dutch oven in deep fat, but they may be fried with a little fat in a hot frying pan. Turn pie often so as to brown both sides.)

Stew dried apples. Drain off juice; mash well, sweeten. Roll pie crust rather thick. Cut circles 3 inches in diameter. In middle of one circle place large spoonful of filling; place another circle on top and press edges together firmly. Fry. Serve with longhorn cheese. Mince meat or dried prunes may be used.

PUDDINGS AND DUMPLINGS

SON-OF-A-GUN-IN-A-SACK

(Hi Pockets taught me to make this suet pudding 47 years ago. Hi Pockets made it a lot, and the cowpunchers loved it and gave it the above name.)

2 cups flour	1 cup bread crumbs
1 cup canned milk	1 cup ground suet
1 cup raisins	1 cup molasses
1 tbsp. soda	1 tsp. salt
1 tsp. cinnamon	1 tsp. cloves
1 tsp. nutmeg	

(Hi Pockets did not use nut meats, but I add 1 cup of chopped nut meats.)

Dissolve soda in molasses, combine flour and bread crumbs to which the salt and spices have been added. Then mix together the dry ingredients with the suet, raisins, molasses, nuts, and canned milk. Mix well, pour into a sack and boil in water for 2 hours.

Serve with FOAMY SAUCE as follows:

½ cup butter	1 cup confectioner's sugar
1 egg	2 tbsp. hot water
1 tsp. vanilla	

Cream butter and sugar, the egg well beaten, and the hot water until the mixture thickens, beating continuously. Add vanilla and serve.

SAYLORS DUFF

(A good steamed pudding given to my mother by her good friend, Mrs. Minnie Diltz, of Sheridan, Wyoming.)

1 egg, beaten with ½ tbsp. sugar, ½ cup Brer Rabbit syrup

3 tbsp. melted butter

1 tsp. soda

½ cup flour

½ cup warm water

Beat well, steam 1 hour. Serve with cream or lemon sauce.

LEMON SAUCE

½ cup sugar

nutmeg

2 tbsp. butter

1 tbsp. corn starch

2 tbsp. lemon juice

1 cup boiling water

Mix sugar and corn starch, add the boiling water and a pinch of salt and boil until thick and clear. Continue cooking over hot water for a few minutes. Beat in the butter, the lemon juice, and nutmeg. Add a little grating of lemon rind.

HASTY PUDDING

(A pudding used by old-time roundup cooks, given to me by Grandmother Dana, an old pioneer of Montana and Wyoming. It is quite easy to make.)

Two cups of hot water placed in the top of a double boiler, with a pinch of salt and ½ cup of sugar. When it comes to a boil, pour $^2/_3$ cups of flour in at one time; beat with an egg beater while cooking, but don't make it too smooth. Should look a little like cooked rice. Cook two minutes. Pour into individual dishes. Sprinkle each dish with nutmeg or cinnamon. Serve with heavy cream. Chuck wagon cooks served it with a dip, but cream is better.

FLIP FLOP PUDDING

1 cup sugar
1 cup fruit, fresh, dried, or
canned; tart fruit is best

2 tsp. baking powder
½ tsp. salt

Syrup

1 cup brown sugar

2 cups water, boil, add 2 tsp.
butter

For pudding, put fruit into a buttered baking pan, pour syrup over fruit. Make thin batter of first 3 ingredients, using water or juice from fruit. Pour batter over syrup and fruit and bake until brown. This pudding will serve six people.
(Recipe for Batter on page 64)

HI POCKETS' BOILED APPLE DUMPLINGS

1 cup sour milk
¼ tsp. soda
1 tsp. baking powder

1 tsp. salt
1 tbsp. lard
flour

Mix milk, melted lard, soda, salt, and baking powder. To this add enough flour to make a stiff dough. Roll on floured board about ¼ inch thick. Cut in 4 inch squares. Put 3 tbsp. well seasoned apple-sauce on each square. Fold over dough and press edges together. Put each dumpling into its own muslin sack. Drop into kettle of boiling water in which there is a rack. Boil 30 minutes. Serve with cream or hard sauce.

HARD SAUCE FOR APPLE DUMPLINGS

½ cup butter
¼ cup hot canned milk
pinch of salt

2 tsp. vanilla
2 cups powdered sugar

Mix together canned milk and sugar, vanilla, and salt. Shape in a cake 1 inch thick and chill. Cut in slices and serve on hot dumplings.

(Hi Pockets could make the dumplings only when near a ranch with a cow, where he could trade for cream and butter. He used white and brown sugar, for he had no other kind; but powdered sugar is best for the hard sauce.)

COOKIES

ROLL DATE COOKIES

Mix as you would a bread dough:

1 cup white sugar	1 cup brown sugar
½ cup butter	½ cup lard
3 eggs	4 cups flour
1 tsp. salt	1 tsp. soda
vanilla	

Roll ½ inch thick. Spread with filling:

1 lb. dates	½ cup water
½ cup sugar	pinch of salt
1 tbsp. flour	

Cook filling until thick. Cool, pour on dough, roll in a cloth, put in icebox overnight, slice, and bake in oven until a light brown.
(This recipe was given to me by an old-time western woman, Mrs. Addie Laman.)

BROWN SUGAR COOKIES

2 cups sugar	1 cup butter or shortening
3 eggs	1 cup sour cream
1 tsp. soda	

Season with cinnamon or lemon extract. Add just enough flour so cookies will roll without sticking. Handle as little as possible. Bake until a light brown.

OATMEAL COOKIES

1 cup sifted flour	2 eggs
1 tsp. baking powder	1 can condensed tomato soup
⅛ tsp. soda	3 cups uncooked oatmeal
½ tsp. salt	2 cups chopped dates
2 tsp. nutmeg	1 cup chopped walnuts
1 cup sugar	¾ cup butter

Sift dry ingredients together. Cream butter and sugar, add eggs, and blend thoroughly. Add dry ingredients alternately with soup, mixing well after each addition. Blend in oatmeal, dates, and walnuts. Drop by spoonsful on a lightly greased baking sheet. Bake in 375° oven until brown. Makes five dozen cookies.

OATMEAL COOKIES

1 cup butter or lard (scant)	1 small tsp. soda
1 cup sugar	1 cup raisins
1¾ cups oatmeal	1 tsp. cinnamon
2 eggs	1 cup flour
5 tbsp. sour milk	½ tsp. salt

Cream shortening, add sugar, eggs well beaten. Mix soda with sour milk, add oatmeal, flour, fruit, and salt. Drop from teaspoon. Bake in moderate oven. Add a cup of broken nutmeats if desired.

CANDY AND ICE CREAM

EASY DIVINITY

3 cups sugar
¾ cup light corn syrup
¾ cup water
2 egg whites

1 pkg. raspberry flavored
gelatin
1 cup chopped nuts

Mix sugar, corn syrup, and water in a saucepan and cook to the boiling point, stirring constantly. Reduce heat and continue cooking, stirring occasionally, until a few drops tested in cold water form a hard ball. Meanwhile, beat egg whites until they fluff up, then add the dry gelatin, beating until the mixture holds a definite peak. Pour syrup into the egg white mixture in a thin stream; beat until candy holds a shape. Pour in a greased pan and cut into squares.

MOLASSES TAFFY

2 cups molasses
1 cup granulated sugar
¾ cup water

4 tbsp. butter
1 tsp. vanilla
⅛ tsp. soda

Cook the molasses, sugar, and water slowly to a hard-ball stage, stirring during the latter part of the cooking to prevent burning. Remove from stove, add the butter, soda, and vanilla, and stir enough to mix. Pour into a greased pan and, when cool enough to handle, pull it into a long rope and cut with scissors into small pieces.

CHOCOLATE FUDGE

2 cups sugar
2 squares chocolate
⅛ tsp. cream of tartar
2 tbsp. corn syrup

²⁄₃ cup canned milk
1 tsp. vanilla
1 tbsp. butter

Mix the sugar, milk, grated chocolate, cream of tartar, and corn syrup. Stir well. Boil to a soft ball stage. Remove from the stove; add the butter but do not stir it in. When lukewarm, add vanilla and beat until it creams. Spread in a buttered pan and when it hardens, mark it into squares.

RANCH ICE CREAM

4 egg yolks
1 pt. good milk
1 tsp. vanilla

4 cups medium cream
¾ cup sugar

Scald the cream. Beat the egg yolks; add the sugar and pour the cream and milk slowly on the mixture, beating constantly. Cook in a double boiler until it thickens a little. Cool, add vanilla, and freeze.

BEVERAGES

CHOKE CHERRY WINE

(This recipe was given to me by an old-time cowman and his wife, Mr. and Mrs. William Booker of Glenrock, Wyoming. He gave me the recipe thirty years ago. At that time he was rodding the VR Cattle Company, which he did for more than thirty years.)

12 lbs. cherries   2 gallons water
6 lbs. sugar

Wash fruit well, cover with the water, and let stand 10 days, stirring and washing the fruit three times a day. Keep in warm place, skimming every day. Strain. Add sugar and set aside until all fermentation ceases. Skim daily. Bottle tightly. 1 tbsp. of pure grain alcohol may be added to each gallon of wine without danger that it will turn to vinegar.
(Chaparral—or buffalo berries, as we Western people call them— may make wine in the same fashion as for choke cherry wine.)

ROSE WINE

A lovely wine can be made of the rosebuds that form on wild roses after the roses fall off. Make the same as choke cherry wine, except run the buds through a good chopper; when you put the sugar in the juice, add one yeast cake.

DANDELION WINE

1 qt. blossoms loosely packed, juice and rind of 1 lemon and 2 oranges, 1 gallon hot soft water. Pour water over blossoms, let stand overnight. Drain. Add lemon and oranges, 2 lbs. sugar. Stir in sugar well, add 1 cake yeast. Let stand one week in a warm room. Strain and bottle, putting corks in loosely.

(This recipe was given to me by my aunt, Mrs. Vannie Jacka. It is very good, and I have made the wine for more than 30 years. 1 tbsp. of pure grain alcohol may be added for each gallon of wine without danger that it will turn to vinegar.)

TOM AND JERRY

(This recipe was given to my husband many years ago by Oscar Thielen as made in the old days when cowmen made their own drinks.)

Use 1 large china bowl and 1 small bowl. Beat the whites of 12 fresh eggs to a stiff froth in the large bowl, add 1 heaping tbsp. sugar for each egg. Beat yolks of eggs separately in the small bowl, add a pinch of baking soda and beat to a stiff batter. Then mix the two batters together, stir frequently so as to prevent the sugar sticking to the bottom.

To serve Tom and Jerry:

Put 2 tbsp. of the above mixture into a Tom and Jerry mug. Add 1 drink (2 ounces) liquor; fill with boiling water. Stir well while adding the water. Grate nutmeg or cinnamon on top, and serve.

COFFEE

To make coffee for a large crowd of people, make it the way the roundup cooks did when on the roundup: Have a large old-fashioned coffee pot. Allow 1 tbsp. coffee to each person, then 1 extra tbsp. for the coffee pot. Put coffee in a thin white sack. Measure water in a cup; allow extra cup of water. Put on low heat and let steep slowly. Let come to a boil when ready to serve. Clear with a little cold water.

TEA

Put fresh water in kettle and heat to boiling point. Allow 1 tsp. tea to each cup of water. Put dry tea in teapot. For a special drink, put 6 whole cloves or 1 stick of cinnamon into the pot with the tea. Pour in boiling water. Let steep 5 minutes.

FRUIT PUNCH

Use 1 quart water, 1 pint fruit juice (orange or any kind of fruit juice). Add water and ice to make 1 gallon. If needed, add sugar. Add a few fresh cherries and 1 pint crushed pineapple. (Makes 1 gallon of punch.)

HOT WASSAIL

Squeeze and reserve the juice of 2 oranges, 2 lemons. In tightly-covered saucepan simmer together for one hour the squeezed orange and lemon halves, 2 sticks of cinnamon, 2 tsp. whole or ground cloves, 1 cup sugar, 1½ qts. water. Strain mixture and add 1 gallon fresh apple cider. Mix all together and reheat and serve hot with crackers and cheese.

(My mother, Mrs. Mary J. Hedgepeth Ash, gave me this recipe, and it is a very good drink for cold weather.)

KITCHEN AND HOUSEHOLD HINTS

To thin icing that is too thick, use a little milk.

To thicken icing that is too thin, use a little powdered sugar.

To keep mashed potatoes warm for anyone late for dinner, place in top of a double boiler and place over hot water. Set on stove over low heat.

To remove paint from clothing, use equal parts of ammonia and turpentine, well diluted with water. Wet the spot 2 or 3 times with the solution, then wash thoroughly with soapsuds.

To keep pickles from molding, place a small piece of horseradish in jar on top of the pickles.

A tbsp. of warm water added to the egg before mixing a cake will make it light and spongy.

When cooking kraut, add 1 tsp. sugar.

Something good which I learned in the cowtown of Belle Fourche, South Dakota: We had shipped some cattle to Chicago. After loading out the cattle, we went to the Oyster House for supper. With the fried oysters they served finely shredded cabbage salted with celery salt. It is very good.

When going camping, take along a few cans of corn (cream style). Fry bacon crisp, then pour out all but a little of the bacon grease. Pour in corn. After cooking a short time, break 3 eggs into the corn and scramble. This makes a good breakfast.

Hi Pockets fried bacon this way: He used a dutch oven but a heavy frying pan will do. Save bacon drippings for this purpose. Fry the bacon in deep hot fat, using the drippings for the fat. The bacon will be crisp, brown, and tender.

In frying potatoes, try making them $\frac{1}{3}$ carrots. Sprinkle a little flour over the potatoes and carrots.

To tenderize an old sage hen or prairie chicken, cut up to fry, slice the breast of the chicken. Soak in a little soda water all night; wash well in cold water, then fry very slowly with a lid over the frying pan so as to steam the chicken.

For a mutton roast, brown well on top of stove, then stick 6 cloves into the roast and roast very slowly until tender. The taste will be more like deer meat than mutton.

When good brown gravy is left from a beef roast, try making noodle soup. Cook noodles in salt water. When tender, pour the gravy into the water and the noodles. Add black pepper.

When packing in on an extended camping trip, take along an old-time yellow slicker. This is the way the old-time cowpuncher took a foot bath when on the roundup: Dig a small hole in the earth about the size of a wash basin, place slicker in the hole, pour in warm water, sit down and place feet in the water.

Ways with fried mush: Boil a pot of yellow corn meal mush, making it thick. Dip a pan into cold water then pour the mush into the pan. Let sit in a cold place to chill; then slice, roll in corn meal, and fry until brown.

To serve over the fried mush, make this:

CREAMED COD FISH

4 tbsp. butter	2 hard cooked eggs
3 tbsp. flour	1 tbsp. lemon juice
¼ tsp. salt	little black pepper
2 cups milk or thin cream	1 pkg. cod fish

Blend fat, flour, salt. Add the milk and stir constantly until thickened. Chop the eggs and add to the sauce with the lemon juice and pepper to season. The cod fish should be freshened in cold water and cut into small pieces. Add cod fish to sauce. Serve in a gravy boat for each to place as a sauce over the fried mush.
(Creamed dried beef may be made the same as the cod fish and also served on fried mush.)

To whip thin cream, dissolve 1 tbsp. unflavored gelatin in 1 tbsp. hot water and add to 2 cups cream; chill for a few minutes, then whip.

Boil a cup of vinegar and a cup of water in a lime-coated teakettle. This will soften the sediment and it can easily be scraped off.

Hints from Hi Pockets:

> To remove rust from a cowpuncher's white shirt make a paste of lemon juice and corn starch. Spread over rust and put out in the sun to dry. When dry, brush off; repeat if necessary.

> A tbsp. of vinegar in the water in which meats are boiled will help to make them tender.

> Sprinkle a little flour over the pan of freshly sliced potatoes along with the pepper and salt. This will help to brown the fresh potatoes.

> Pour boiling water over oranges and let stand 5 minutes. This will cause the white lining to come away with the peeling when the oranges are to be sliced.

> To scale fish more easily, dip fish first into boiling water, then scale in usual manner.

TOILET AND LAUNDRY SOAP

Soap was made by almost every ranchman's wife. Many years ago, while living on a large cattle ranch which my husband was rodding, I learned how to make this best homemade soap I have ever used.

Take 15 qts. soft water, 9 lbs. beef tallow or other grease, 2 cans concentrated lye, 1½ lbs. rosin, ½ lb. borax. Mix these ingredients together and boil about ¾ hour, or longer if necessary. After it cools just a little, pour into a wooden box, cut into bars when set.

For toilet soap, make the same way only use beef tallow. When it cools a little, add some peppermint oil for odor. If wished, beat for a short time with an egg beater. This will make a lightweight toilet soap.

HEALTH HINTS

Fifty years ago people lived so far from the railroad and doctors that in case of illness the old-timers had to use the things nature provided. Raised in North Dakota a hundred miles from doctors and a railroad, I learned many things from the old-timers, cowpunchers, and roundup cooks. Here are a few which I find as good today as I did fifty years ago.

For chills: Pick the leaves of the wild native sage, wash, put a cup full on back of stove, pour boiling water (about 3 cups) over the leaves and let steep 30 minutes. Drink hot, stay in bed, and keep warm with hot water bottles.

For boils: To draw or bring a boil to a head, we gathered some native cactus, burned off the spines, then washed cactus in warm water. Lay cactus on a board and mash to a pulp, put the cactus pulp on a piece of cheese cloth. Warm this poultice in the oven, then place on the boil. We used this for man or beast.

For gall bladder colic: Try 15 drops of fluid extract of dandelion in a little warm water. It often works like a charm.

For hoarseness: Mix 1 tsp. glycerine with the well beaten white of an egg. Add juice of 1 lemon and enough water to make palatable.

For hiccough: 5 drops camphor dropped in 1 tsp. sugar.

For sore throat and hoarseness: A towel wrung out of cold water and bound to throat with dry towel. I find this is very good and that it will help one to sleep when ill with sore throat.

For a good hand lotion:

25¢ gum tagracanth	4 ounces glycerine
1 ounce toilet water	4 ounces witch hazel
juice of 1 lemon	1 qt. soft water

Soak gum tagracanth in soft water overnight. Beat all the other ingredients into this with an egg beater. Store in small jars.

NEW RECIPES
April 1969

FLIP-FLOP PUDDING BATTER

1 c. flour	1 T. sugar
1 t. baking powder	1 T. shortening
Pinch of Salt	

Enough water to make a batter the consistency of hot cake batter.

SOUTHERN BISCUITS

2 c. sifted flour	1 or 2 t. sugar
4 t. baking powder	1 egg beaten
1 t. cream of tartar	1 c. shortening
½ t. salt	$^2/_3$ c. milk

Mix dry ingredients. Work in shortening. Add beaten egg and milk. Bake in hot oven.

POTATO CANDY

$^2/_3$ c. mashed potatoes	⅛ t. salt
½ c. peanut butter	1 lb. confectioner's sugar

Mix and press into buttered pans. Refrigerate before cutting.

variations

If desired, 2 t. cocoa may be added.
Also, if desired, a roll may be formed and rolled in finely ground nuts or coconut, refrigerated and sliced.

POTATO PIE

2 c. evaporated milk
Add 2 eggs beaten
¼ t. ginger
1 t. nutmeg

2 T. Molasses
Pinch of Salt
1 c. sugar
1 c. mashed potatoes

Mix as for pumpkin pie. Bake at 350 degrees for 30 minutes. Then test with a knife.

POTATO-FUDGE FROSTING

Potato-Fudge Frosting makes a good, easy-to-make topping for angelfood and sponge cakes.

To cover a 9-inch tube cake, melt ⅓ cup of butter or margarine and cook until lightly browned. Add 2 squares of unsweetened chocolate and stir until melted. Stir in ⅓ cup of mashed potatoes, 1½ teaspoons vanilla extract, a dash of salt and mix well. Gradually blend in 3 cups sifted confectioner's sugar and 2 tablespoons of milk. Beat after each addition.

POTATO DOUGHNUTS

Ingredients

1 c. mashed potatoes, un-
    seasoned
3 eggs
¾ c. sugar
3 T. shortening, soft

2¾ c. sifted flour
4 t. baking powder
1 t. salt
¼ t. nutmeg
1 t. mace

Method

1. Prepare potatoes as directed on the mashed potato mix package for 2 servings; (1 cup)—except omit the salt.
2. Beat eggs well. Beat in sugar and shortening.
3. Sift dry ingredients together and stir in. Stir in potatoes.
4. Chill dough 2 hours. Turn onto generously floured board. Roll ⅓ inch thick.
5. Let rest 20 minutes. Cut with doughnut cutter.
6. Fry in hot fat (370 to 380 deg. F.) until brown. Drain on absorbent paper. Serve plain, sugared or glazed.

INDEX

73